CATULLA ET AL

Tiffany Atkinson was born in Berlin into an army family and has lived in Wales for many years. She is a lecturer in English and Creative Writing at Aberystwyth University, and edited *The Body: A Reader* (Palgrave, 2004). She leads regular writers' workshops and academic seminars, as well as giving many readings throughout Britain and internationally.

She won the Cardiff Academi International Poetry Competition in 2001. Her first collection, *Kink and Particle* (Seren, 2006), a Poetry Book Society Recommendation, won the Jerwood Aldeburgh First Collection Prize and was shortlisted for the Glen Dimplex New Writers Award. *Catulla et al* (Bloodaxe Books, 2011) is her second collection.

TIFFANY ATKINSON

CATULLA ET AL

BLOODAXE BOOKS

ISBN: 978 1 85224 888 8

First published 2011 by
Bloodaxe Books Ltd,
Highgreen,
Tarset,
Northumberland NE48 1RP.

www.bloodaxebooks.com
For further information about Bloodaxe titles
please visit our website or write to
the above address for a catalogue.

Supported by
**ARTS COUNCIL
ENGLAND**

Cover design: Neil Astley & Pamela Robertson-Pearce.

Printed in Great Britain by
Bell & Bain Limited, Glasgow, Scotland.

For my friends

ACKNOWLEDGEMENTS

Thanks are due to the editors of the following publications in which some of these poems have appeared: *Agenda, English, Fragments from the Dark: Women Writing Home and Self in Wales*, ed. Jeni Williams and Latéfa Guémar (Hafan Books, 2008), *Identity Parade: New British and Irish Poets*, ed. Roddy Lumsden (Bloodaxe Books, 2010), *New Welsh Review, Poetry International Web, Poetry Review, The Warwick Review* and *The Writer in the Academy: Creative Interfrictions*, ed. Richard Marggraf Turley (Boydell and Brewer, 2011).

Warmest thanks are also due to Neil Astley, and to my friends and colleagues in Aberystwyth.

CONTENTS

I

Catulla

If you are reading

this will have been for you
Cornelius
        of the high end kind-
nesses of libraries and smoking-rooms

your diamond window flung wide many
thousand storeys elsewhere
        I kept all your postcards I'm
        the one who took your nicotined
        Catullus   also at your leaving-
do I pinched your silver ashtray and for all
                your generosity

this late handful of leaves   Do you
read me
        old friend
              overandout

Catulla

Well, Rufus, here's a talent
for the inappropriate
to make the tawdriest suburban dogger blush –

and after all these months
as single as a bar-stool.

It's not enough
that you look less at me
than at a passing bicycle

but still I make a case for you:
how suddenly you so surpass
the local streaks of piss, my friends
ring all the haddock-handed lads
and hit the pubs without me. I

must hear how you leave women
fired like bows in hotel rooms
across the city, yet despite myself
I keep my health, I will grow old –
a clever woman wouldn't die of feelings, merely.

Love, I wish you were ridiculous.
Best you never meet my friends –
who in their cups would tell you
how I starved for weeks and wandered
through the streets in borrowed dresses,
bless, aflame for an encounter. Dear

god. May you never know
how slow unlovely women burn,
nor how we keep our heads down.
Sod you. All the books say I must
break this at the stem. Live long,
die happy. Take these petals as they come –
for kisses, curses, kisses.

Rufus's Dog

So it takes the whole poem
to imagine his dog. The dog
was in his study when he called –

and no commandment she can think of
takes a stand on the imagining of dogs.
Across the rug it yawns with heimlichkeit,

a muscled bag of hearth-warmth. Just
his fingers, where the skull collects the spine's
chords, lift the muzzle's blunt love. But

that's animals. Crossbreeds, she knows,
are fickle when it comes to instinct. Over
rolls this demijohn of fealty, open as a palm.

Exquisite, how the skin takes touch. The eyes
roll back. The universe contracts. And she
observes the soft jewels of the genitals

for she is known for thoroughness. It's
an oldish dog, but not dead. In the pistons
of the hips lie all the casual cruelties of fuck –

she sees the outraged neighbour storming
from her kitchen with a bucket of cold water –
get that mad hound off my Mitzi! Awkward

teacups afterwards: the wunderkinder pups
some brutal husband dunks into the rain-butt.
All the bevels of his no-good-boyo head against

her knee, his steady heat as dreaming tears him
fanging over plains. Where the ribcage clasps
a wolf's heart. People thinking she's the cat sort.

Another moon song, Rufus

Two, three, four –
Anyway, love's nothing
like the moon. The moon's
a drag. A passive-aggressive
in a better woman's dress. The one
you find outside your house, at 3 A.M.,
in tears, wanting to *talk things through.*
The moon has issues. She won't lighten up,
that botoxed princess who, in private, loves
to play the psycho at the high school dance –
how casually she shakes the blood from
her corsage and limps home barefoot,
smoking! Then she hacks her mama
into bits. And all day long the girl's
been starving, or a-bingeing, or she's
scratching at her face. And she'll
outlive us all, the chilly bitch,
she'll outlive all of us…
And *one* –

Clodia

e.g., we are the only two in town who
smoke these cigarettes. I cannot learn too much
of her. Like migraine: fascinating, hurtful,
larger than oneself.

How does hate swing through fixation into love,
or something like? So if she drives past in the
family car I want to part the traffic
like a sea for her –

which is confusing, at the very least. She
stirs some belly-bowl of kindness not quite mine.
How many indiscretions does she know of?
Every one, of course;

and Sunday afternoon means she's across town
with the children, all the family to lunch.
The banter flies. I scrub the cooker, wash clothes,
keep a life ticking.

A late wasp guns its engine at my window.
It is dark before I let it out to face
a firing-squad of stars. And nothing quite puts
distance like the stars.

Her husband left me green with want, she knows that.
But I'm sick for something further back. Look: I'm
the stickyfingered brat still clamouring at
the apron, whining.

RIP Rufus's Dog

Animal lovers   pet
keepers and misanthropists   clatter
your million feeding-dishes with a loud
                                      spoon
Rufus's dog   that tupper and
worrier   knicker-sniffer   brother-
in-kind   old *paterfamilias*
                        is dead
Whose feral odour lingers still in corners

Dear to Rufus as his own back teeth
                                Who
never knew a leash except to chew
clean through it   whose opinions
could be heard three streets
                        downwind
Begetter
        of a piebald clan of home-
wreckers   and clear-souled as his livid
breath was foul
                has slipped the hand
that nursed him through incontinence
and pushed his whiskered snout
                        into the one
dark   It would take a narcissist
                        indeed
to measure loss by species
                        Rufus calls
with whiskey breath   and mud to the knees
of his trousers   Just the salt wind
                        stinging his eyes

American Teeth

Egnatius returns from his 'business
trips' with whiter teeth each time.
He curls back his lip like a horse. *See
how I've been flossing on the diamanté
thongs of starlets*, *flash*. In truth
it's more like looking at a freshly minted
graveyard. No gods could be vainer;
then again, they don't grow old. Poor
Egnatius: every time he grins, his face
can't help prepare itself for lightning.

Basia mille

Then live with me, Rufus.
We'll have four fine rooms
and an excellent kitchen

but knowing what night does
we'll probably starve. One
can measure out one's span

by letting x be kisses minus t
until. Let any fucker work us
out who hasn't better business

for their small hours. Meanwhile
kiss me in the checkout queue
and let the tight mouths clatter –

scandal's for neurotics and they live
on small change. Kiss me then, as
daylight follows to the power of

Bi

I hate / I love / I
cannot grow apart
the black/red bloom
of one blood root that
forks and burns
/and burns

Antiromantic

Sometimes you meet half-
way, all flowers and good
trousers. Or I flick myself
after your heels through
the tightening streets like

running each day nine ten
eleven miles for the rollicking
heart is real. Like rain. Some-
times the sky's the only one
with a clear take on things, did
n't you say that, didn't you?

00.52

Give it up, Catulla! Take the sea for its
easy amnesia; the car, its intimate
monoxides – why hang about? Your work could be
done by a monkey;

no family to speak of; and most friends would
be elsewhere – networking, accepting prizes,
dropping off the kids, out shopping, getting laid.
Consider the blade

in the boutique-scented bathroom, gentle drifts
of paracetamol, the empty bottles
at a photogenic angle, all your small
affairs in order;

back, back to the still, white centre, quiet as
a pill. It's just an exercise in self-will.
You might do worse than think about it, lady:
all you could let go.

Aurelius

handsomely preaches non-attachment.
Catulla grows smooth as a pebble,
as an old spoon, as a grey Jag E-type,
as a new hand. One elastic band

tight on her left wrist, to remind her:
take less. Ask for less. Desire's like
hair: the quotidian, impossible fixation.
She has left her hair. She finds she's

grown quite thin; has always *wanted*
to be thin. A paradox? Aurelius says
a woman has no business doing logic.
Until then she'd let him win at chess.

And Rufus's youngest, ASBO-boy,
whose hot-wire skills are known through
seven counties, leads the after-school-club's
weekly Meditation On The Pure Heart!

Mentorship, they call it. Leave him well
alone, you half-cut Saesneg kiddy-fiddler,
was how Rufus put it to him outside
Dempsey's. So she heard. And just like

that, was freshly smitten with his total,
solar inability to give a shit. You know,
the stylist said, while touching up her roots,
your hair grows even when you're dead.

Dear Kate,

Weekend pavements are for pale girls. All the milk-
fed daughters of our town are out, their neon
eyelids flashing. They are scaring cats
and setting off alarms –

are brazen with their cigarettes and tampons,
passing lip-gloss round with strips of teeny pills.
Absurdly fluent in their kissing. Always
kissing, oh, someone –

and Rufus, strolling on the promenade, says
hello, Kirsty. Jess, you're looking stunning. Sam!
I almost didn't...when did you become so...?
What a cult of shrieks.

But later, when they clatter past in tears, or
carry injured seagulls home in chip-cartons
or share a fag-end on the prom, I cannot
stop to think of them

at our age: thickening in the cul-de-sacs
of clapped-out marriages – worse – dessicating
over spreadsheets. Which side are we on now, Kate?
P.S. Coffee? Soon?

Micra

Catulla climbs into her small
black car. It rattles like a seed-pod.

She is still surprised by how few
of the real poets drive. She herself

has ferried most of them through god-
less intersections to atrocious hotels.

But she loves the pram-upholstered
traps of cars, their quick escapes. And

nine years up and down the learning
curves of motorways have proved

that lovers in the rear-view aren't that
close. She's rolled a thousand cigarettes,

peeled oranges, changed clothes, cried,
slept and written books behind the wheel.

And now she plucks her teenage nieces
from the queasy swell of sirens at a piss-

up. She is sober at the mast-head
as her little craft is tossed from lens to lens.

And who'd replay the footage of two
drunk girls lurching from the kerb into a car,

catching behind them, through a fizz of light
pollution, Castor & Pollux, the Dioscuri?

Poetry wars

Potayto / potarto, Sestius. Avant-
garde indeed. I've got handbags
with more counter-culture in. You

who scoffed a hot fish supper
off my book then blogged about it
to the gods; who'd scalp your readers

for their pillow crimes for holding
words like like like like like roses ashes
in the mouth for hiraeth schadenfreude

agápē etc and the poor old-fashioned
self a freshly severed ghost. Or do
we shake the same chains, Sestius –

you're at my shoulder with the other
hand. Out there the same moon, trees,
however many million million mouths.

99

Iuventius, your corona of red hair
makes my fingers itch. I've wondered what this means.
You sat behind me; I was cross-legged on the
carpet like a girl

and everyone was singing for a birthday.
Leaning back I felt your breathing on my neck.
A bottle got kicked over. We were sober:
wine too 'sour' for you

and I, as usual, driving. Skin long starved
of touch can grow obscenely sensitive – don't
you know that yet? Because I learned that as a
teenager myself.

I had my handful of smashed glass; your hair burned
hard against your temples as you leaned in. Girls
will find your prettiness unnerving. You kissed
me, Iuventius,

you did. It was impartial, like a burn. I
felt the small sting of your curiosity
as salt livens a cut. I have no answer
for your cool, soft mouth

although eventually you'll bite off heart-
break sure enough, which won't be matronly, nor
cut you slack for all your many charms. It's the
original bitch.

Each time I shifted gears as I drove home I
thought of you. How women may be brought to this.
I gnaw through what's between us. You could be my
child. Go forth then, kid.

The main attraction

That is the pier:
>   *esprit de l'escalier*
>>   held up with spray
and starling shit. All night it rocks with
dancing. Furius treads the tinder of the old
boards swearing blind he sees the lights

of Dublin, he's that tight. Someone's
wife stacked up against him like a pin-
ball machine
>   and the one he came with

smoking at the railing as the sea
lays tactful napery between the groynes:

she's humming new york new york
>>   want to –

thinking how the mud would clam
the eyelids shut and tense its wriggly fingers.
All the little mouths would suck like dead stars.

It's a bridge with cold feet.
>   Wake up
someone's bawling as she steps back on
to mapped land, in the city that never.

27

Domus

Sawn-off city, why have signs,
when only tourists need signs

and the body tilts its soft retort
towards the sea? Days, weeks,

many Christmases. Here
are seagulls who have learned

to pick locks. Here is weather
like a wasp trapped in a glass.

High wind talks you through
the fault-lines of the house –

look what you've gone and
married, with your small inher-

itance and single woman's toolbox!
Here's a grinning key, and here

is subsidence. Half a mile away
the sea makes passes darkly

at the coast road. Yesterday
a beaked fish swung like a piñata

in the cherry tree. There's no
such fish on Google, though

it fries up beautifully. From
the garden you can sift the bay

through cupped hands. It is calm,
and twin moons flash like hemi-

spheres of one mind. Tomorrow,
in that lifetime, you'll be home.

Ave atque vale

But that's how it was in the old
world – all its stars and seasons
in cahoots. The lucky burned
clean up in wars and loves –
their ash fell thick and cooled

a continent. The rest of us sat
tight and by and by new gods
rolled up; glad-handed pamphlets
under doors, left drifts of cheap
cologne in stairwells.

*

                                  Attis
for example: there's a name
you don't hear much at parties –

poor frenzied boy who split
his own sex at the root

and woke a lost, forked creature
swaying palely in a ring of blood –

let's raise a glass to that;
to Ariadne's tangled grief

refreshing daily with the tide;
Aegeus at the look-out plunging sea-

ward like a jeroboam... O heroes
brides nymphs oreads kings

gods and demigods!
A pang, a dazzle, glimpsed like

nipples or the whites of eyes
in slack suburban twilights, O

*

like aren't we so ironic these days
lucky us

*

Meanwhile a wedding –
remember – with turrets and a wine
cellar and catacombs; a girl

who let the apple roll
to the foot of a blond-haired stranger,
and wars, always wars;

the din of kitchens
and the TV on three youths
in regulation tracksuits

standing round an ancient loom,
a woman with a *listenup*
demeanour saying something like

let axis a be time apportioned
and let b, the shuttle in your free
hand, leave a map of how desire

tugs bright against it. Colours
branch like corals; cymbals flutes
and bunting through the avenues

and always someone weeping
down the dry horn of a telephone.
The guests disperse,

the mountains kick a moon out.
Who was the man with the gold
mane blowing smoke rings –

what was the offering? Theseus
walks out to meet the beast,
poised between death and celebrity;

a woman folds her house down
frame by frame and dead-
heads all the fairy-lights, for

this was a garden for lovers.
Cats make their bids from
the flower-beds. She walks

out empty on the coast road.
What a good ship grief is,
bringing us
                each to her island.

Hymen Hymenaeus

All for the sun which was
       the first sex
       coaxing into motion
every protein every mineral each cell
       Hymenaeus Hymen Io!
       Io! Hymen Hymenaeus

        *

So to the cooling of salt
       at the temples
       and the pale foot
bruising the grass   To office workers'
       bare arms spreading
       picnics in the lunch-hour

all the loosened ties
       of Keppel St and
       builders whistling
don't pretend you don't know girls
       it's old rules when the trees
       release their pheromone

        *

One for the boy awkward with books
       and violin case   Oh
that bobtail of white
knicker in the sports hall   how it
       flickers just behind
       his closed eyes

One for the bag-lady pushing
       her trolley of cats
       down a dangerous pavement
to pick the municipal hyacinths
       three four five   yes
       each of her darlings

One for the auspices of starlings
      The jogger who stops
      as a hearse rolls past
to tilt his dripping forehead
      his breath held
      close like a torch

        *

And here is the wedding
      whose bride steps out dazzled
      whose groom steps out dazzled
down to the sea through the petals
      Hymenaeus Hymen Io!
      Io! Hymen Hymenaeus

        *

One for the queenly ovum
      in her hive of cells
      for the ticklish seed and
fosterers and donors and the white-
      coated harvester
pacing her glittering clinic

Oh bed in which all

.   .   .   .
.   .   .   .
.   .   .   .
.   .   .   .

      and at the white foot of the bed

        *

All for the night-feed and death-watch
      For the budded hand
      and teaspoonfuls of breath
The moon in its sling turning slowly
      Hymenaeus Hymen Io!
      Io! Hymen Hymenaeus

Notes

The poems in the *Catulla* sequence take their departure from specific Catullus poems as follows (from *Catullus: The Poems*, tr. Peter Whigham; Penguin Books, 1966).

If you are reading: CATULLUS 1

Catulla: CATULLUS 8 AND 11

Rufus's Dog: CATULLUS 2

Another moon song, Rufus: CATULLUS 34

Clodia: CATULLUS 51

RIP Rufus's Dog: CATULLUS 3

American Teeth: CATULLUS 39

Basia mille: CATULLUS 5

Bi: CATULLUS 85

Antiromantic: CATULLUS 70

00:52: CATULLUS 52

Aurelius: CATULLUS 21

Dear Kate,: CATULLUS 58

Micra: CATULLUS 4

Poetry wars: CATULLUS 22 AND 44

99: CATULLUS 99

The main attraction: CATULLUS 17

Domus: CATULLUS 31

Ave atque vale: CATULLUS 63 AND 64

Hymen Hymenaeus: CATULLUS 61

II

et al

Celibates,

eh? Keeping ourselves
like pieces of Quaker furniture.

Don't knock it.

Want

Its freak arpeggios
and avatars. Extortionate,
like fleas. The twelve-bar shtick.
For thinking I was well-rid.

Rocking all night on the jamb of sleep.
And the heart's a dirty stop-out.

Soft machines

That gentlemen's watch
on you, stripped minimalist

sits like a collar on a snake –
its crisp links on my inner skins

wherever your braced wrist goes
a fresh machine. Our soft assembly-

lines, our infinitely geared cogs
and couplings: every night's invention

startles, jangling the whole house
with its quanta. Each atomic proposition

meets its yes-girl. Love's a bootstrap
physicist, and we both cynical from habit,

yet we wear these ordinary skins like blue-
prints, proofs of an originary genius.

Italian cars

is a compound noun, test-
osteroid fired from the hip

with all the nouveau glam of sunset.
Mad for horizon, you are. Those

are our ghosts at the bus stop,
breathing our tyres' hot sugars –

our bodies braced like diamonds –
far-flung and barely affordable.

What kind of woman adores the ar-
peggio of gears? I'm the real Medici

and what we don't know about drives,
o tesoro mio, put your bright foot down.

Why I am not a Buddhist

Also the problem of anger;
its dopple drive-bys – like

a siren at its closest point
is PERSONAL
                          it screams in
through an open window
of my calm house and now
                          whose

is this bog-wall language
in your pretty schoolmouth?

To bed on a quarrel is rats
in the basement.
                          Shouldn't
we give up our home
and set forth from our country –
the Sons of the Buddhas
          all practise this way. Be-

loved my books and my
costly white walls and my jewels
in soft boxes my anger

Marzipan blues

Later he tries to explain
the turquoise joy, at ten,
of that first Rangers strip;
his birthday-fingers skidding
on the wrapping's brittle ice.

It's occult, such a shock
of cloth – the sweet, sheer blue
enough to make his teeth ache.
Hard to bear the perfect interval
of white trim at the neck: the brisk

heroic V whose yearning geometry
fits *just so*. It's a humbling ratio,
along the lines of football: stadium;
wee boy: the goals of men. But he's
already elsewhere. And of course

he thinks I wouldn't understand:
I'm pointing like a school-marm
everywhere but at myself. Look –
was the blue like this? I say. Or
this? Well, was it? Anything like this?

Bad karaoke

The wedding night of my second trip
to Scotland   two-by-two of us propping
up the bar of the Kilmarnock Travel-
odge in something less comfortable

which happens to be karaoke night
in these heels   All day shy as a tree-
frog in my patterned dress and now
the whole room glitters   Even my true

love says I shouldnae feel I have tae
as I launch my high notes at the tone-
deaf anaglytpa   If the make-up runs
it's just I haven't slept since Thursday

and I've lived on crisps for three days   Only
dinna make me drive home on a hangover's
slipped gears   the sun on my forehead past
Dumfries   still asking why indeed   Delilah

Love of the bones

Just so you know, if you don't,
should you be signed into the ground
ahead of me, I'll come alone, but

once the Goth kids have gone home,
before the insomniacs come out
to smoke among the headstones

and before the morning joggers
or the other women come in state.
I'll reach you with my rabbiting

spade and sundry kitchen tools,
and being of robust build, prise
your casing open – as didn't I

always, love – salvage a little
something, like a hand – your left,
the one with the ring and the tremor,

which should disengage quite sweetly
at the distal wrist crease. I'll take
its dry weight in my lap as if you dozed

beside the radio. I'll warm it through
the life-line to the private ambers
of the fingernails. I'll lay it on its back

and stroke its palm. I'll press the finger-
pads against my smarting eyelids and
anoint its glove of skin until it gleams

right through like old wood. I'll wrap it
in my mother's scented handkerchief,
for miracles. When your ring falls clean

off and grows bright again, I'll thread
all twenty-seven tender bones to jiggle
at the skin beneath my blouse. After

that, if I don't hear from you, I'll open
windows, let the rain in. Travel, maybe.
Learn a different language. Move on.

Princess; pea

Some welcome that was:
black-and-blue to breakfast
where the prince refused to pass

the butter and the queen spilled
scalding coffee on her wrist. As
if it wasn't obvious. Contusions

high as heraldry, the bed-wetting –
pure Romanov. So Lev was right:
the aristocracy are stupid. Six weeks

scrimping from the folk who'd hate
her as she'd hate herself in their shoes,
she could eke that pea out into broth

enough for five. The feather-beds
themselves are hurtful; just the silver
on the table makes her faint. It did

take everything. She calls herself
Natasha now; her blood runs red.
These marriage-plots – she'd laugh

if that would bring the house down
on their soft soft hands, their
minted vowels. She hides her small

face in the pillows and she howls.
Seven basic types of story, said her
enemy, who nonetheless hid books

inside her sewing-box. And who's
tobacco is it that she smells, recalling
that – his or her father's? Both had

auburn hair though that's irrelevant,
historically. It's the present which
insists, hard and green in the soft palm

as. She's commandeered the kitchen.
Mummy's boy is stitching coins into
the bolsters while his mother gobbles

bank-notes. There are queues back
to the village well. She stirs the pot
and laughter flies like bullets.

Piper

How unexpected,
that through all that din, their
untuned ears still field his tiny
music! O they leave behind

such *silence*.
He has seen whole families
felled by it in less time
than it takes to run a bath

while implication
gathers body like a fugue,
the playground's taped,
the parents broadcast tight

with shock,
the posters fly up. Every time
it is the same, and not the same.
He thinks, *of all things, loss is*

the particular,
although, time was, folk swallowed
grief like all things quite
beyond them, and still mustered

grace
to be unfazed when little Hans
returned, say, in the form of singing rock,
or learnèd pig, or soft, propitious rain –

because, of course,
the child has been there all along.
Like music. No one ever thinks to say
of music, it was there and then

it was not.
They just listen harder. Listen.
Generations fizzing through
the inner ear's dark sea, like stars.

Grassholm

the magic of one of the world's largest gannet colonies, close up.
PEMBROKESHIRE BOAT CHARTERS

When the gannets turned her flesh
into a gannet, all the light blew in
at once. It sucked her skyward, shrieking.

He squinted from the stunned deck.
She was wheeling like a sycamore-
key. He had witnessed childbirth,

and the indivisibility of pain, here,
too, was hurtful. Her mother's name
was what she cried out last. But chaos

mends. Then there she was, all china-curve
and braced wing, and a beak he thought
unusually expressive. He ran cold fingers

down her spine and knew the bones. Thrilled
with the common speech of touch, they spoke
in elemental terms that he would later publish

to acclaim. He passes seasons by himself
and reads the Mabinogion and Ovid. Calm
surprises him. He comes home from long visits

in the summer months with eyes like rock-pools.
She'll have given him Sistines of seabirds,
plummeting parabolas of love. And he'll

have oiled and preened her feathers and her
blue feet – though it makes him faint, to feel
the quickfire of her heart and breathe the ocean

of her. Change like that must ruin ordinary
folk. These two far from ordinary, neither
knows who gained the greater freedom by it.

The Secret World of Michael Fry:
1st Policeman

There was the car chase (thirteenth
take), the drugs bust and the teen-
star's webcammed overdose, so who

was filming when the 1st policeman
quit his post to take up residence
in Aberystwyth? The costume seized

like daydream. One pint in The Cooper's –
gratis, Sergeant – and he knew he'd nailed
the powers of conviction. Out he staggered

with a skinful and a theme tune,
all the local bastards banged up and
a sizzle through the pay scale: slap–bang

into Christmas. He was comical with hidden
gifts. It really looked like snow. His wife
was writing cards – oh darling, how do you

expect me to keep track of all our friends! –
the racket upstairs just a flock of daughters
in and out of bedrooms like *matroshki*,

full of self, the youngest still a print of him –
same heart-shaped face and freckled hands –
so pretty he recalled some poignant but

instructive episodes about sex education,
series three. Beyond the kitchen window
something snagged the hazel tree. He thought

that it put distance in a funny way. It stared in
like a refugee and had another name for him.
It was a needy apparatus, dragging light. He

ran through all six series, couldn't place it. Then
his wife, whose name rolled slowly like a gold
ring down the drain, pulled blinds down on

a sudden sandstone tenement. He recognised
those sirens; women's voices crackling through
glass. He'd deep breathe through the ad break,

start again. Cue music. Let the snow fall. Here
he comes, the good cop wreathed in smiles, no
foot put wrong, who knows his house by moonlight.

Chicken Little

So I lift your dress
and kneel before your bruises –
each a corsage; plural,

formal as a marriage –
thinking, this is how the story
stiffed you. Acorn, my arse.

It's my job to hear the whole she-
bang: the who did what to whom
with what, and how the sky itself

was gunning for you. Most of all
I want to hear how everything
seemed lost – how hard it hurt,

how long, and where, precisely.
Incidentally, you're more than
averagely beautiful. I do believe you.

You must name it, sweetie. It is
only pain. Which isn't a punch-line
in the therapeutic sense, but then

we're archetypes, not Notting Hill
neurotics – and besides, I mean to crack
your pretty neck. I do the fox. It's nature.

After Bluebeard,

two years after, she can stride
through almost all the castle's corridors
and is fine. Fine. No one can
recall such frequent hunting parties,

springtime festivals and healing fields.
Her sister climbs the tower
as the waste ground clears itself –
the ratty polythene and slashed tyres

peeling back on rich lawns, perfect
for the summer's reading circles. She
has opened all the rooms and smelted
every key but one; and this a meditation

on the stain that runs clear through her
like the letters through a stick of rock.
She can't bring herself to ask just what
it is about her that unlocks another's

horror-chamber. There was his blade
at the strop of her throat, the unexpected
breeze of French cologne. His weight.
And once again, she's pushed out wings

and drifted up. Her crown nuzzles
the ceiling. Now the whole outrageous
kingdom must dissolve. It's like...
It's like... But that is the business

of dreams. She's on the beach;
bare feet, a borrowed wedding-gown,
grains of sand beneath her fingernails.
All fears, all pebbles, have their inner,

secret names. Her brothers,
leaning on the sunset, sow the sea
with skimming-stones. Look, husband.
The astonishing impartiality of light.

Rain –

It started unremarkably,
like many regimes. We sat like children
making quiet things indoors. The rivers

burst their staves and soaked the folds mid-
country; they were schlepping people out in pedalos,
and punting through cathedrals saving cats. One lad

clearing out his granddad's drain was still caught
when the waters lapped the record set in *1692*.
Imagine. News teams donned their sombrer cagoules.

The house had more floors than we knew. In twenty years
we'd never spent so much time in one room. I'd no idea
you had a morbid fear of orange pips, or found French novelists

oppressive. On the seventh day, completely hoarse,
we took to drawing on the walls and staging tableaux.
In delirium all actions feel like role play –

protein strands against the ooze, the animals we made –
and rain, a steady broadcast on all wavelengths,
taught us everything we know about the tango. Only

when we grew too thin for metaphors was rain just rain.
We thought about the drowned boy, how he watched
the lid of water seal him in, for all his bright modernity.

Was it a Monday morning when the garden was returned,
tender with slugs, astonished at itself? Our joined hands
were the last toads in the ark. We walked; we needed news.

Philosophy

came down to which end of the knife
you found yourself at. Not much
reading after that. You took work

in a kitchen: chop and slice,
the tendons flickering in your wrist,
grappling for a handle on your old self.

Friends mean well – they mean it
as a compliment, but *hold your head up*
as opposed to? Once a slattern,

now you keep your surfaces so clean
an incident room could pick a finger-
buffet off them. Infrared, keypad, fish-

eye, mortise, night-latch, deadbolt,
door-chain, hinge-screws, Chubb &
sliding-double-action-lever-lock

enough? You might as well ask if a kettle
tells the truth. And kitchens are duplicitous –
the news is full of cutlery. Statistically,

it's someone you think you know.
Stay in. Stay out. Spend fifteen minutes
on the lintel with your keys hot in your fist

and do the homework. Kitchen tables are
the abstract form of family banter. Steak-
knives make us better hosts than monkeys.

Chairs, in general, share a get-up-when-you-
want-to-get-up outlook. Twine's for make and
mend. Hot buttered toast is unequivocally kind.

Fiacre

(Patron saint of gardens)

Such a cold year frost through
April in the gardens that I tended
all the young wives fed me like a child.

Foxglove for example roars
up through the cold like hunger
like a feeding cry god's hand
the pulpit grows out of the ground.

Tight of words but loosened as a rain
on turned earth I was that man
sorcerer they said or showed their secret
bodies for the miracle and walked
out under dark without a word.

Pain the garden and the flesh a small
bird never mind Whose wings lie folded
in the breastbone quick & dead are no-
one's property nor rain the opposite of gold.
For heart a momentary fist of mud
and all its creatures o lord in the end.

Philology

First, you write how heat
is like another body on your back:
you're losing years each day by way of minerals.
They teach you to drink Coke with salt in
for the sweating.
                        Certain things seem close to home –
there's always someone on the hunt for something new
to say about the moon, and everyone keeps chickens,
but you can't get butter, never mind a European paper,
and the language is a minefield.
                        Sixteen nouns
to hold the shapes explosion makes of civic space:
all derived from ancient artists' names. An Institute
which manages the rhetoric of pain. Its scholars
are exempt from service but (dear god)
they're thin. To reach its top floor you must climb
from brute hurt, through the drab, split-
levelled middle-management of trauma,
to the triple-glazed panopticon where dons
plot points of suffering so fine they're whistled
through closed lips. To hear that language
is to lean so closely in a man might kiss
or cut your throat.
                        You find no word for *coast*,
for all that you smell salt at nightfall. And
you've lost your ID in a skirmish at the archives
so you'll have to trek inland. The letter
handed round for nineteen days says, underlined,
how [untranslatable] you miss the bloody seagulls,
strutting round *sans papiers*. And starling-storms,
above the pier in safe, safe Aberystwyth.

Portrait of the Husband as Farmers' Market

The husband is a mud-on-the-boots philosophy
in old jeans, loving nothing so much as slow growth.

His thoughts are distinctively British cooperatives,
jovial stall-holders subbing each other loose change.

His chest is a trestle laid with rare meats, smelling
of the smokehouse, his belly a seed-loaf, knotted

and oddly exotic. The sex of the husband's a plump
trout, a one-off, lolling silverside-up in its shine

for a wife with the eye of a magpie. His heart,
apparently a leafy crop, is a loom of many rhizomes

reaching furlongs – who knows how far? The husband
is mineral-rich, irregular, leaving scraps of himself

all over the street for starlings to pick at. Is a crowd
of bright skins in a bushel, wheels of feral cheese,

impossible brews from the ditches. Is the season's
measure, taking the weather however it turns out.

Thunder at Saxmundham

The train grows with festival heat
as I read the work of a man
I slept with at The Bird in Hand –

separate rooms but yes it crossed
my mind; these steam-pressed rape-
fields in their high bell jar of sky –

the lowlands make me louche
I text my husband, tasting candour
like a strange fruit. The engine

idles at a junction; this is the poet's
aubade for his lover. Someone closes
windows on the live air. Buddleia

in the siding shakes its tacky dildos.
Any minute now the sky will fall point
blank on silos and conservatories, on

the whole world. It's a poem: there
is nowhere else to look. And here's
the body, like a creel of bees. I bang

against the glass: look up, people.
First comes lightning. All the kids count
elephants. The poet teases stresses. *Now*.

Class of '86

Sister Mary Mag was telling how
a third of the earth was burned up

a third of the trees were burned up
and all the green grass. Gail Novak

née Delaney says now over canapés
she pushed the cursor of the ouija

board. The name of the star was
Wormwood and Chernobyl burned,

the foxes shrieked like martyrs
in the Surrey rhododendrons and

a third of the waters turned bitter.
Down where the train-tracks cut

the hockey fields the third angel
sounded his trumpet and a great star

blazing fell. We swallowed its light
with our bones and all the sprigs

and blossoms of our M & S nighties
wormed into our skin. Sister Gen

said later she had leapt from bed for
sure a wolf had got in. Textbook mass

hysteria said Dr Quick the prickarse
did he feel youse up as well says Gail,

which wasn't as bad as the ouija or
our shadows on the dormitory wall.

Why Dad Can't Return to His Old House:

Way too full of wives
and step-kids, step-grand-kids,
a malicious thickening of in-laws.

No obvious third-act crisis.
A swerve off the M25
for a cottage on Dartmoor

where only the woodstove knows its place.
He stencils the passage of stars
on the skylight, and lives like a geranium.

Blood-child and immune,
I move through his moods like a surgeon.
No one calls. I'm unimpressed.

The photos are stashed in the loft
and the TV's off. The things he likes
to look at all point outward and away.

There's space in the cupboards
for mystery. For making peace with other
lives; with women, even, maybe.

Hardy's Tragedies

The socio-economic problems of
  his pocket perhaps, these up-
  country London ink-pot fellers

The social problems of
  the brighter endurance
  of women in these epochs, time
  closed up like a fan before him

The religious problems of
  zoophytes, mollusca, shellfish
  then he perceived with a sense
  of horror that it was *himself*

The ethical problems of
  here's a mouthful of bread and bacon
  that the misses have sent, shepherd

The bio-philosophical problems of
  a sunless winter day emerged
  like a dead-born child

The spiritual problems of
  cuckoo-pint – like an apoplectic saint
  in a niche of malachite

The sexual problems of
  sheenen curls, and plenty o' em
  Staining her hands with thistle-milk
  and slug-slime Weren't I stale in wedlock
  afore ye were out of arms? Say you do
  now, dear, dear, husband; Say you do
        now I have killed him

Ballad of Three

To dinner with my oldest friends:
    he's pissed. She's never late.
He banters, eyes strung to the door –
    I scrutinise my plate.

She kisses him, but on the cheek –
    that's for my benefit,
and when she orders for them both
    he's having none of it

then orders just that. Bloody hell,
    what marriage does to people –
and if tit-for-tat in things like that
    is life together, equal –

frankly I'd die single. But
    until the food arrives
we make a stab at catching up
    while toying with our knives,

and all this time he knocks it back
    and waxes sentimental –
although his hand (twice) on my knee
    does not feel accidental.

Friends, you look tired. The dinner's dead –
    pass the salt. In the usual manner
a part has come loose in the tender machine
    with me left holding the spanner,

and I no natural fatalist:
    still, walking home, I notice
more than the usual incidence
    of dead gulls, kids on crutches –

Slim excuse to smoke till dawn,
    indulge in solo drinking,
then resist the urge to ring them and
    for christ's sake, say I'm thinking

how you've umpteen ways to skin a cat,
    still more to rock a boat –
The stitch in time might save your hat
    but make you leave your coat.

Anatomy Exhibition Visitors' Book

Wow. Awesome. Plastic, they
don't really look like flesh. Just
meat, nameless meat. Gross.
Meat. Dried out. It was really nice
but sad. I hope they are in heaven.
Awesome. Like meat. Humbling.
Thank you. They do look human
when you see the fingernails and
things like that but other parts –
they still look plastic, obviously.
Wow. The mysteries under the skin.
I loved the show so educational! I
am unafraid of any future operation
I may need. Very instructive –
but lacking in emotion. Wow. It's
changed my life for the better I
will never smoke again. Incredible!
Oh my God, these are really dead
people. How do you cut this bodies?
Vital for medical students. Totally.
A beautiful way of celebrating what
it means to be alive in the 21st C. IT
WAS FANTASTIC I WOULD LIKE
TO GET MARRIED IN THERE. Under
the shell of our skins our bodies are so
similar, regardless of skin colour. I am
AMAZING after all. Maybe should have
photos of the people when they are alive?
So moving!! I love human body!! Plastic.

Small hand

(for G)

Beach–crumbs
from your small hand's

frill of fingers as you try the punch–
line of a million miniscule

genetic propositions:
                                first step
since the great-great hand of species

swung its dull bulb from the tree canopy
and snatched the dropped fruit. Whole

new cities open for you overnight
where gods if gods push infinit–

esimal hands like snowflakes
or quarks through windscreens

& committees & return you each
time palms out ravenous and upright.

According to

Once, about the time you start to notice trees
and he found out his wife was not his wife
in any sense but name, Elijah took the dog,
two apples from the sideboard, and went out.

Not long afterwards, he came upon an old friend
bent beneath the bonnet of his car, cursing
every sprocket of combustion engines. What
do you suppose the point is? asked Elijah.

And the friend replied, I have to be there.
Throw your spanners down and come with me,
Elijah said. And so the friend did. And his name
was Tomos, after whom he never thought to ask.

And Elijah was amazed. Next there was a daughter
which, close up, they didn't know. But Tomos said
she looked a lot like his girl would've had she lived.
He split one apple threeways, and the girl laughed.

And her laugh was as a pocketful of loose change,
as the moment when you down your pint and dance.
Her name was Manon. She was heading to the clinic.
Then she got her mobile phone out. Mam? she said.

So from there they went north, telling stories. Till
they came upon a farmer, bitter drunk, for all his fields
had failed. They listened, picking fruit seeds from their teeth,
and where those fell sprang cider-presses, booming.

Soon a crowd came out to see what had been happening.
I killed a man, said one man, looking thin. Shit happens,
said Elijah. Sell your house, give all the money to his folks
and walk with us. The man did. He gave nobody his name.

Meanwhile the crowds grew till there wasn't room
to slide a slice of toast between them. Tomos asked,
what's this about then? And Elijah said, just as you
left your hurtful car to walk with me, so this lot feel.

Look at the rhododendrons! They don't give a toss
about the funding cuts, the polar bears. They do
their own thing. Throw your keys into that hedge,
ignore the cameras. Be your own true kicking self.

So Tomos did. He was a simple man, and able
to draw truth like tears from anyone. Elijah said,
you know the way that pressure-regulating valves
secure the rear-brake lines for heavy braking?

Tomos nodded. Well, Elijah said, you see, that's you.
At this the grief beat out like crows, and Tomos felt
a hatching in the space, of light. Elijah felt it too. And
where they left a third, unheard-of apple, grew a hamlet,

grew a village, grew a town, where people started over
hopefuller than all the Born Again Virgins of America.
These are the words of Manon, set down with the baby
on her knee. Elijah Tomos, he'll be. All this happened.